THE WORLD OF THE
WHALE

Written by
SMRITI PRASADAM-HALLS

Illustrated by
JONATHAN WOODWARD

wren
&rook

For Chris, Céline, Nina and Eloïse – S.P-H.

For all those in my pod, old and new, who make the journey worthwhile – J.W.

First published in Great Britain in 2018 by Wren & Rook

Text © Smriti Prasadam-Halls, 2018
Artwork and design © Hodder & Stoughton Limited, 2018

ISBN: 978 1 5263 6064 9
E-book ISBN: 978 1 5263 6065 6
10 9 8 7 6 5 4 3 2 1

Wren & Rook
An imprint of
Hachette Children's Group
Part of Hodder & Stoughton
Carmelite House
50 Victoria Embankment
London EC4Y 0DZ

An Hachette UK Company
www.hachette.co.uk
www.hachettechildrens.co.uk

Publishing Director: Debbie Foy
Senior Editor: Liza Miller
Art Director: Laura Hambleton
Designer: Claire Munday

Printed in China

Every effort has been made to clear copyright. Should there be any inadvertent omission, please apply to the publisher for rectification.

The website addresses (URLs) included in this book were valid at the time of going to press. However, it is possible that contents or addresses may have changed since the publication of this book. No responsibility for any such changes can be accepted by either the author or the publisher.

LIST OF CONTENTS

JUST LIKE US

Inhabiting an underwater world of wonder, the whale is a giant of the deep.

Diverse in species and size, it varies from the playful dolphin to the majestic blue whale, the largest creature on Earth.

And yet, though whales may dwell in the heart of the ocean, each one of their kind relies on the same air that humans breathe; they are mammals, just like us.

Their world is one of mystery, from the seasonal pull which guides them to cross thousands of kilometres to give birth in the same place, to the strange sounds and songs captured in their intricate calls of communication.

BREATH OF LIFE

Coming up for air, they exhale high into the sky. They breathe deeply through their blowholes before diving down once more. Perhaps they will hover briefly below the surface; perhaps they will stay submerged for many minutes. But they will eventually burst up again to take their next breath.

Whales are mammals. Long ago, their ancestors lived on land, but over millions of years, their bodies adapted so that they could live in the water. Still needing to come to the surface of the ocean to breathe, they use their blowholes. Sometimes single, sometimes double, blowholes enable whales to breathe deeply and fill their mighty lungs.

SKILFUL SWIMMERS

Their prehistoric ancestors may have walked on land, but whales are perfectly suited to life in the water. Several physical adaptations have given them both style and skill at sea.

SKIN

Smooth, rubbery skin with an oily surface helps whales to move quickly underwater.

STREAMLINED SHAPE

However immense in size, whales are sturdy, sleek and fast. Their slender bodies glide easily through the sea.

FLIPPERS

A whale's flippers help it to change direction and balance, so that it can swim with skill and confidence.

STRONG MUSCLES

A whale powers through the ocean with the help of a huge mass of hefty muscles that moves the fluke up and down.

FLUKE

Each whale's fluke – or tail fin – is unique, like a fingerprint. The fluke propels the whale through the water and helps her to dive. It moves in an up-down motion, unlike the side-to-side motion of fish tails.

BLUBBER

Layers of fat, called blubber, keep whales warm in polar seas. Blubber is also an excellent way of storing energy, which is particularly useful when whales go on long migratory journeys.

WHALE FAMILIES

Whales belong to a group of mammals called Cetacea. From small, darting dolphins to enormous humpbacks, there are many different species of whale. We organise them depending on whether the species has teeth or baleen plates. Within those groups, we then put species into families that share similar features.

BALEEN WHALES

These whales have two blowholes and catch their fish by gulping enormous mouthfuls of water. Instead of teeth, there are plates of comb-like bristles – or baleen – inside their mouths, which act like a sieve to capture shoals of tiny fish and krill.

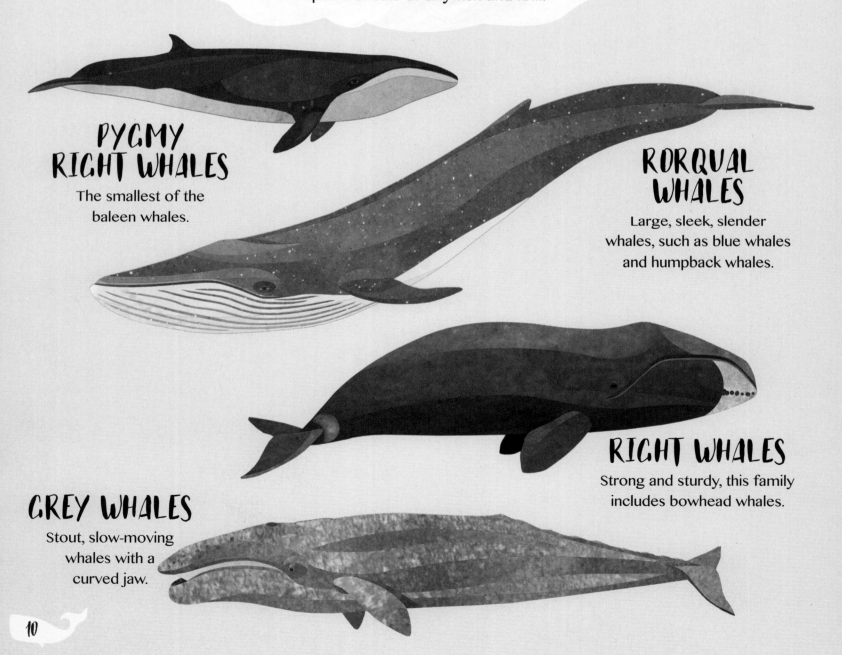

PYGMY RIGHT WHALES

The smallest of the baleen whales.

RORQUAL WHALES

Large, sleek, slender whales, such as blue whales and humpback whales.

RIGHT WHALES

Strong and sturdy, this family includes bowhead whales.

GREY WHALES

Stout, slow-moving whales with a curved jaw.

TOOTHED WHALES

With a single blowhole, toothed whales are hunters, using their teeth to capture prey. They are usually smaller in size than baleen whales.

BEAKED WHALES

A large family with at least 21 different species, including the southern and northern bottlenose whales.

DOLPHIN FAMILY

The largest group of whales, which includes orcas – also known as killer whales.

SPERM WHALES

This group includes the massive sperm whale, largest of the toothed whales, along with the much smaller dwarf and pygmy sperm whale families.

NARWHALS AND BELUGAS

These whales have distinctively curved heads, rounded flukes and are small and stocky in build.

PORPOISES

While very similar in shape to dolphins, porpoises have a less pointy beak and flatter, rectangular teeth.

RIVER DOLPHINS

These dolphins dwell not in the sea but in many of the world's great rivers, from the Amazon to the Ganges.

11

UNDERWATER ECHOES

Whale sounds are varied and complex. They are used for navigation and for communication and are distinctive, unique and memorable.

Toothed whales, such as pink Amazon river dolphins, have developed a remarkable ability to find their way through dark waters using high-frequency clicks. Known as echolocation, these clicks bounce off the whale's surroundings and return as an echo, revealing the size, shape, material and position of nearby objects.

The deep melodic tones of baleen whales keep them together on vast migratory journeys, even when separated by kilometres of ocean. These long, low lullabies travel over four times faster in water than in air and send messages to keep the whales close. They may tell of fish to be found or predators that lurk ahead; we cannot say. For now, these messages are secrets of the sea.

THE SONG OF THE HUMPBACK WHALE

A haunting, wistful song echoes through the ocean. Regular patterns of notes resound, as the tune of the humpback whale rises and falls. Building and repeating, over and over again, the soulful song can continue for several hours.

Many believe the humpback whale's beautiful song is a male's mating cry, while others suggest it is a challenge to ward off competition. The sounds range from low burbling wails and moans to high-pitched howls, resulting in a range of sounds that are the most varied in the whole of the animal kingdom.

The melody is passed on, picked up and performed by all the male whales within the area, which is often a vast expanse. Each whale repeats the refrain, resulting in an oceanic orchestra whose song captures the very heart of the sea.

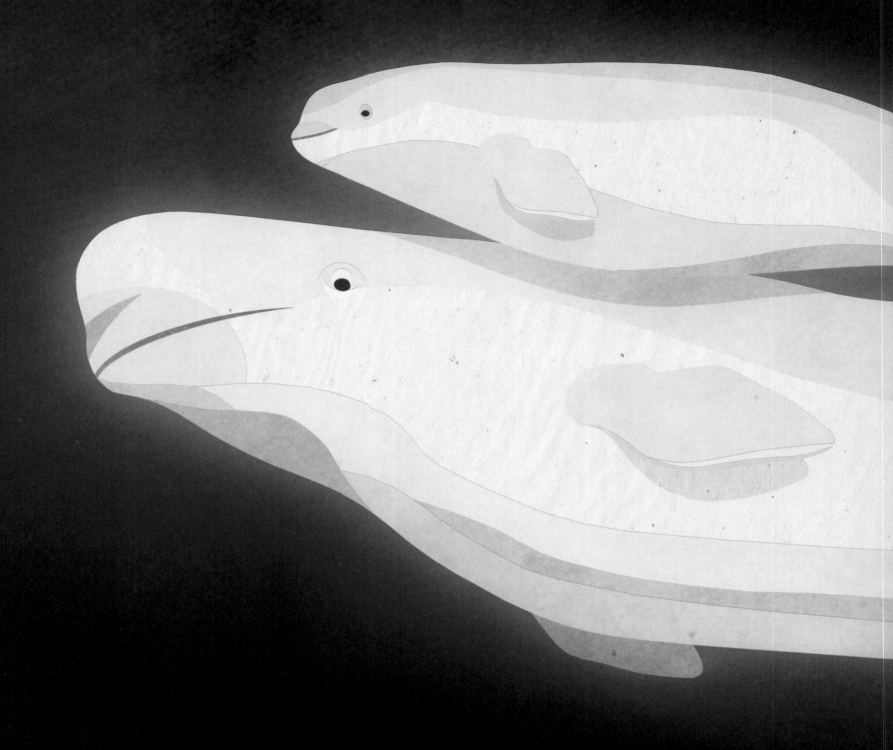

SENSING THE OCEAN

Dwelling in the murky deep, with only a faint glimmer of light to lead her way, the whale has senses finely adapted to her needs. Her eyes, small and alert, dart into the dimness. Equipped to reflect back any light, her eyes allow her to see by day or by night, above water and below it.

But sound will serve her better than sight in this underwater world. Her ears, tucked inside her head, decode the tell-tale vibrations that echo back to her across the sea and alert her to the presence of predators and of prey.

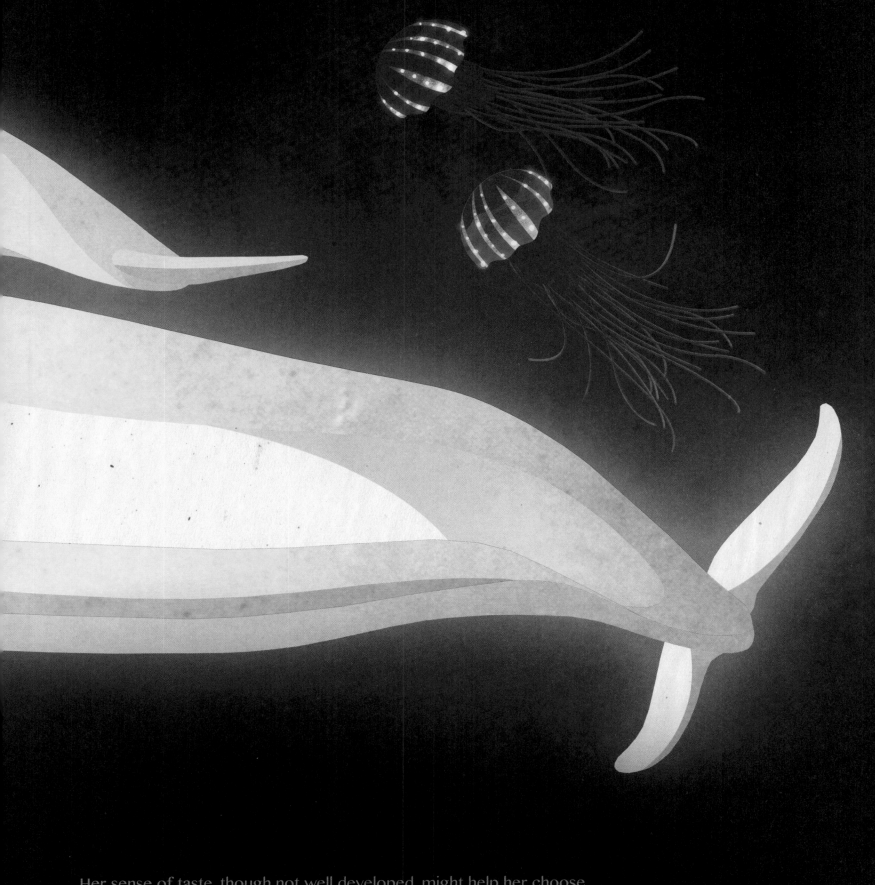

Her sense of taste, though not well developed, might help her choose one type of fish over another. Her skin, sensitive to the touch, allows her to bond and show affection with gentle rubs and nudges.

Alert and adept, she is perfectly attuned to her surroundings.

SILENT SIGNALS

Whales can signal emotions from aggression to compassion, grief to curiosity. They communicate with an assertive, eloquent body language, from gently skimming the waves with a partner to slamming down hard on the water's surface.

BREACHING

With a mighty lunge, the whale lifts from the water. For an instant, time stands still as his enormous body is suspended. Whether a warning or a courtship display, his message travels across the ocean.

SPYHOPPING

The whale surfaces above water, a striking vertical streak. Keenly, she observes her surroundings, always alert for prey and danger.

TOUCHING

Nudging one another with tender touches, mother and young travel side by side. Bumping bodies and swimming closely, they bond through gentle, affectionate gestures.

LOBTAILING

Lifting fluke or flipper from the water, the whale slaps as hard as he can against the surface. Perhaps the resounding crash echoes with aggression. Perhaps it warns of danger ahead.

THE DANCE OF THE DOLPHIN

Dipping and diving, cresting the waves and leaping lightly, dolphins are like a troupe of dancers in unison. With friendly faces and mouths naturally curved into generous smiles, these graceful acrobats breach and flip with elegance and ease.

Energetic and playful, they blow frothy bubble rings for fun, chase one another, snap jaws, butt heads and are frequently spotted riding the waves next to a boat.

But playfulness conceals clever motives in these sharply intelligent creatures. Leaping, jumping and swimming alongside ships conserves their energy, allowing them to reach speeds of 30 kilometres per hour.

Their unique signature whistles and frequent synchronised movements give a glimpse of the highly social lives that dolphins lead.

IN THE POD

A pod of whales crosses a wide sea. Distance may seem to separate the members of the group, but they are never alone. The pod's methods of communication reach over and under the surface of the sea, keeping contact close. No matter how deep they dive or how far they roam, the whales travel as one.

Though some baleen whales are solitary by nature, toothed whales are known for sociability, preferring to live, feed and travel in the security of a pod.

While mothers dive long and deep for food, other females care for the young calves, keeping them close to the water's surface. Small groups of whales are known to stay together through bonds of companionship and co-operation, even though they are unrelated; loyalty can extend beyond family. Some pods remain together for a whole lifetime.

Scientists have discovered that whales have a culture of their own. They communicate with different dialects and accents depending on where they live, just as we do. What are the underwater secrets that they whisper to one another? Perhaps, one day, we will unravel the language of the whale.

TOGETHER

The moment he emerges, tail first into the world, she gently nudges him
to the surface for his first breath.

Day by day he grows bigger, bolder and braver. Her milk is the only nourishment
he needs. For his first year of life, he rarely leaves her side. He swims in her
slipstream and rests when she rests.

His stamina and strength grow as he watches and waits, listens and learns.
Mother and child, always together.

She is his shadow upon the shimmering waters of childhood. Careful. Constant.
His guardian and his guide.

Together, they roll and they ride. Together, they twist and they turn in the tide.

Always together.

THE LONG JOURNEY

A pod of grey whales has spent the summer feeding on the abundant fish and krill of the freezing, polar seas. But these waters are too cold for breeding, so as winter approaches, the whales head off to warmer waters. They begin a voyage of many thousands of kilometres. Once there, some will mate; others will give birth and bring up their calves beneath the shelter of a sunny sky.

When spring arrives, the sleek swimmers begin their return trip.
Their young are strong and ready for the challenge, but they
must learn to build stamina. Their mothers have not eaten for
many months and long to feast on fish.

Who knows how they find their way? Some believe it is the pull of the Earth's
magnetic force that guides them home, while others say their map is written
in the contours of the seabed. Swiftly they swim.

At last, the pod of whales reaches its journey's end: back where it began.
The whales return to a world of cold, Arctic beauty. A land of snow and
ice, and a sea sparkling with silvery shoals of fish.

FAR AND WIDE

Each year, humpback whales across the globe undertake an epic oceanic journey.

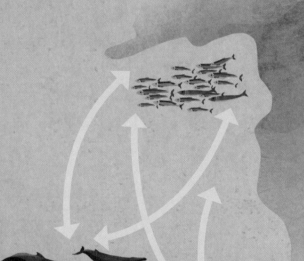

NORTH AMERICA

PACIFIC OCEAN

ATLANTIC OCEAN

SOUTH AMERICA

KEY

 Breeding grounds

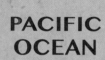 Feeding grounds

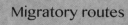 Migratory routes

Migrating from icy summer feeding grounds, they journey to warmer breeding grounds for the winter, where they can raise their calves. For some this will involve an incredible round trip of as much as 20,000 kilometres.

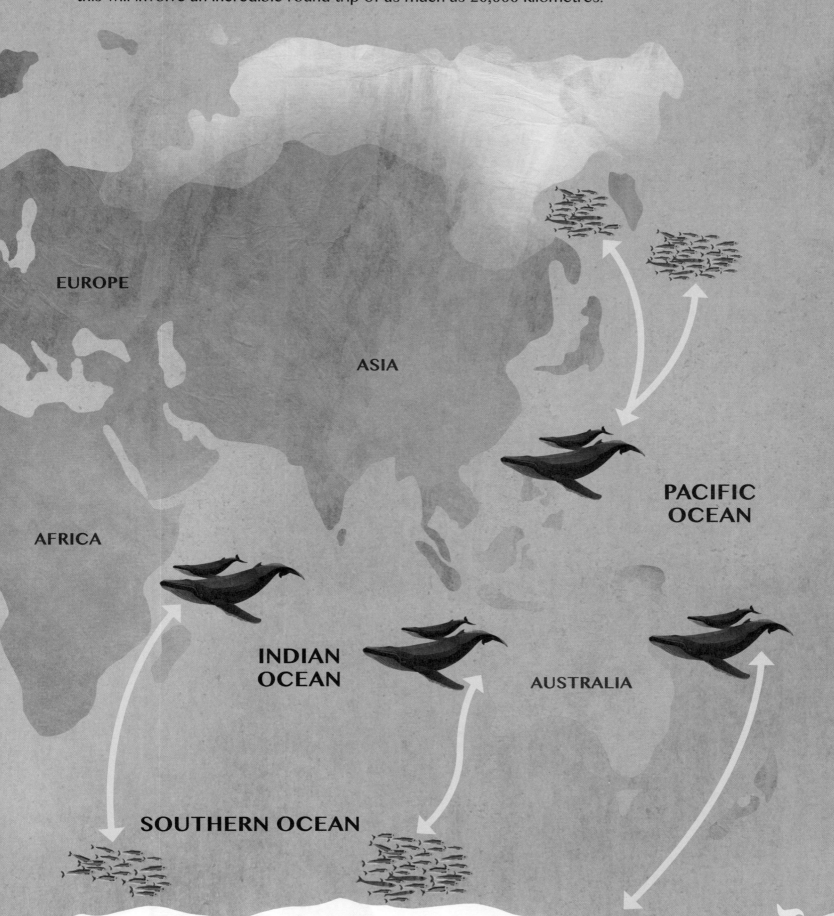

EUROPE

ASIA

AFRICA

PACIFIC OCEAN

INDIAN OCEAN

AUSTRALIA

SOUTHERN OCEAN

LARGER THAN LIFE

Nothing stirs. The sea is still. And then a shadow fills the water. An immense presence, glimmering beneath the surface of the sea, catches the day's last lingering light.

The largest living creatures on Earth, blue whales can measure 30 metres long and weigh more than 180 tonnes. Their vast, elegant shape is synonymous with the majestic beauty of underwater life. Hunted widely in the twentieth century, many of their number vanished and they remain an endangered animal to this day.

Consuming enormous quantities of krill, each whale needs a large area in which to feed. Perhaps this explains why they so often keep their own company.

FORAGING FOR FOOD

Trawling the ocean, scouring the seas, whales are often on the hunt for food. Whether capturing prey alone or gathering in groups, they are master feeders.

BALEEN WHALES

Trapping food in the fine fingers of their fringed baleen, these whales are filter feeders. Scooping enormous gulps of ocean as they swim, they catch small fish and krill in their baleen to feed on, while forcing water out.

Sometimes they catch prey in a cascade of burbling bubbles, which billow from their blowholes. By blowing bubble-nets, as shown here, frothy foam traps the prey, allowing the whales to surround the fish and dive in to feed.

Simpler still, baleen whales sometimes roll on to their sides and suck up prey from the ocean floor.

TOOTHED WHALES

Listening to the whispers of the waves, toothed whales frequently use echolocation to find their food. Sometimes they round fish up into a group known as a bait ball and feed from it. Or, they herd fish into shallow water to be caught with ease.

These whales often hunt together in groups. Their diet is broad and can include squid, octopus and – in the case of the orca – marine mammals. Always listening, they watch and wait – hungry and hopeful.

DEEP THINKERS

Curious, creative and – above all – clever, whales are masters of the ocean, famous for their large brains and impressive intelligence. Inquisitive and alert, they possess a human-like ability to learn new things, rarely found within the animal kingdom.

Whales have created complex techniques of communication, problem-solving and play. They have also mastered cunning methods of hunting. Dolphins have developed the practice of fish stranding, where prey is chased on to land, captured and eaten – with just enough time spare for the hunters to be swept safely back to sea.

A whale's intelligence does not rest with her alone; the knowledge she gathers is passed on to the next generation.

KILLERS AT SEA

In striking suits of black and white, orcas are instantly recognisable. They are a formidable force: their more familiar nickname is the killer whale.

Few marine mammals would survive an attack. Equipped with fearsome teeth and powerful tails, orcas have an appetite for fish, birds, seals, sea lions and even other whales, including those much larger than themselves.

Fiercely loyal, family means everything. Hunting in pods of up to 40 members, they remain closely linked to their own, often for life. Cruising cold, coastal waters, they communicate using sounds instantly recognised by their clan. They co-ordinate hunts and attack together, even pursuing their prey on to land.

Swiftly swooping in for the kill, these whales are a deadly pack of predators.

DANGER, DANGER

At one time, humans hunted whales relentlessly for their meat, oil and blubber in a practice known as whaling. While whales are now protected by international laws, some countries still insist on pursuing these beautiful creatures. They are tracked, trapped and killed.

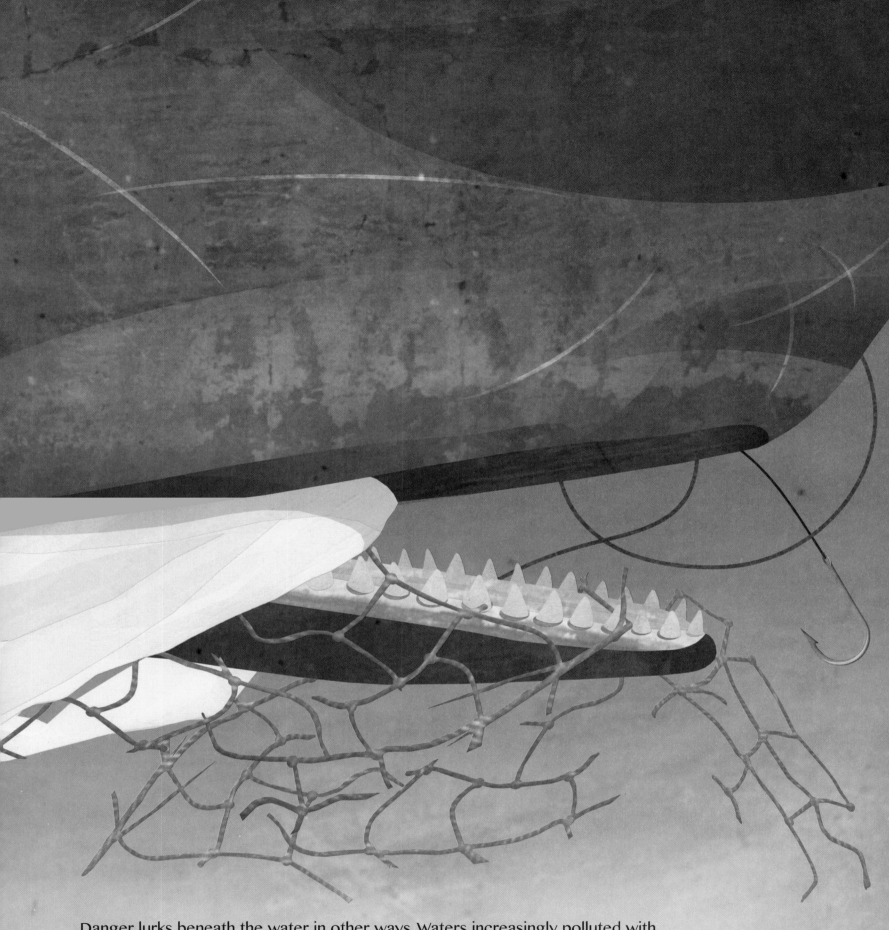

Danger lurks beneath the water in other ways. Waters increasingly polluted with chemical spills, waste and plastic packaging threaten to destroy the precious home of the whale. Meanwhile, the natural sound of the sea is becoming contaminated. The marine industry, boat traffic and military activities emit high levels of noise into the sea. Since whales rely on sound to travel, communicate and feed, this noise pollution can be deadly.

WATCHING WHALES

Attracted by their playful, friendly behaviour and wide-mouthed smiles, people are keen to see whales and dolphins for entertainment. A large industry keeps the animals in captivity for amusement parks and shows, visited by millions each year.

However, whales need to live in the wild. Those in captivity have often been removed from their families; confined to tanks, they are unable to travel the long distances they usually do. Many captive cetaceans become weak or ill.

Happily, there are better ways to see these magnificent creatures up close. Whale watching is possible from land and from sea, so whales can be viewed living in their natural habitat, wild and free. Many whale-watching companies are part of conservation projects and are run by marine biologists.

AS OLD AS THE SEA

The bowhead whale patiently patrols the Arctic waters, watching history unfold. His long life connects us with centuries long gone.

Some bowhead whales are known to be more than 200 years old; they have lived through decades of progress and transformation. It is incredible to imagine the changes that have shaped the world across their lifetime: remarkable advancements, but also increased pollution and loss of wildlife.

A BALANCING ACT

Whales play a vital role in the ecosystem of the ocean, helping to sustain much marine life. The large amount of food they consume helps to keep the marine food chain in order, ensuring that certain types of sea life do not overpopulate the ocean and cause an imbalance.

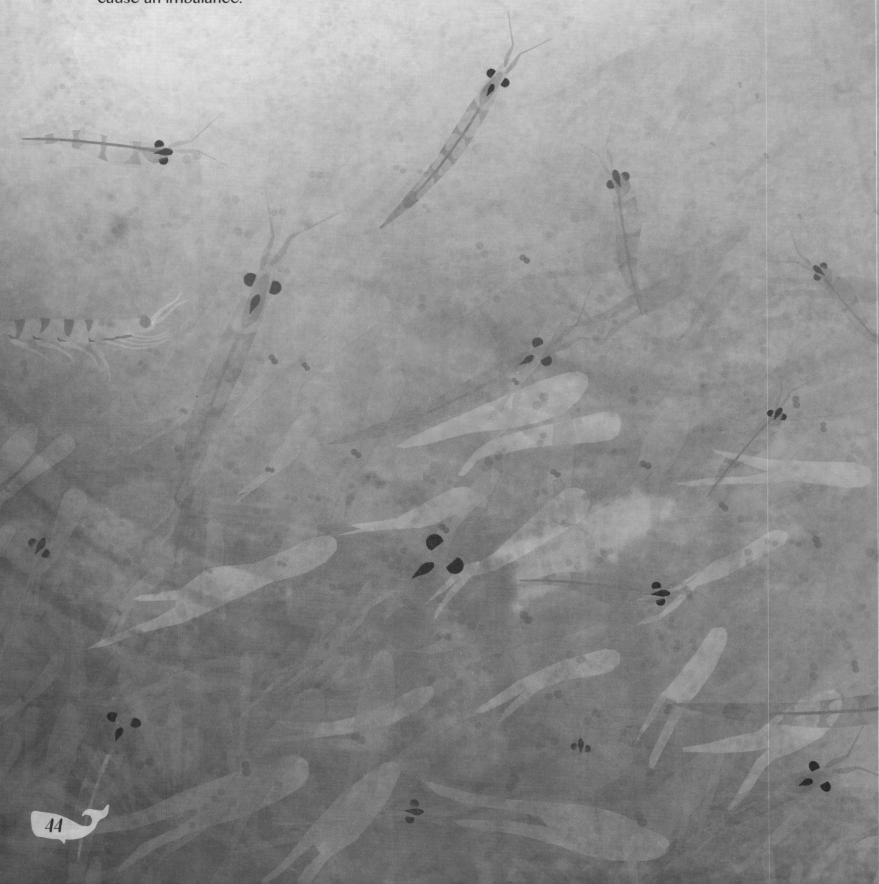

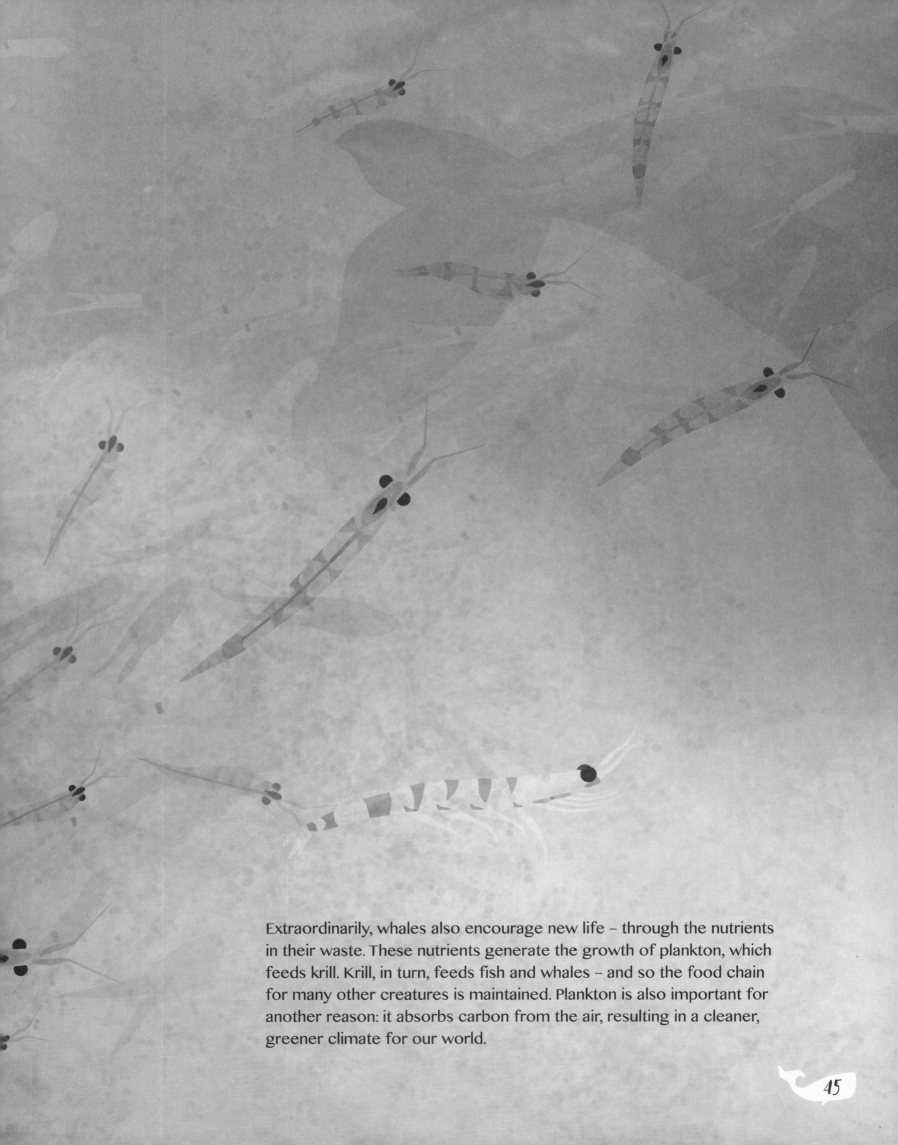

Extraordinarily, whales also encourage new life – through the nutrients in their waste. These nutrients generate the growth of plankton, which feeds krill. Krill, in turn, feeds fish and whales – and so the food chain for many other creatures is maintained. Plankton is also important for another reason: it absorbs carbon from the air, resulting in a cleaner, greener climate for our world.

SIZE MATTERS

Whales vary greatly in size, from the tiny porpoise to the vast blue whale.

Human
1.7 metres
0.07 tonnes

Blue whale
30 metres • 180 tonnes

Pygmy right whale
6.5 metres • 3.5 tonnes

Sperm whale
18 metres • 56 tonnes

Pilot whale
6.5 metres
5.5 tonnes

Orca
8 metres
4.5 tonnes

Bowhead whale
18 metres • 75 tonnes

Narwhal
5 metres • 1.6 tonnes

River dolphin
2.4 metres
0.1 tonnes

Northern bottlenose whale
9.8 metres • 7.4 tonnes

Grey whale
15 metres • 35 tonnes

Harbour porpoise
1.5 metres • 0.07 tonnes

Beluga
5 metres
1.3 tonnes

Hourglass dolphin
1.8 metres • 0.09 tonnes

Humpback whale
16 metres • 36 tonnes

SAVE THE WHALES

It is remarkable that our sea-dwelling neighbours help create better air for us to breathe. It seems only right that we should treat these graceful creatures with the dignity and respect they deserve. One big way we can help keep them safe is to be environmentally friendly, so that we preserve their habitat as much as possible.

We can also support the efforts of whale conservation charities, which are working hard to protect whales in the wild and to free captive cetaceans. The leading charity in this area is WDC, or Whale and Dolphin Conservation. They are working towards a world where every whale and dolphin is safe and free. You can adopt one of their orcas or dolphins, helping to give these amazing creatures a happier future, on their website: **uk.whales.org**.

INDEX